T0354857

PIECES
OF ME

Melissa Monék

authorHOUSE®

AuthorHouse™
1663 Liberty Drive
Bloomington, IN 47403
www.authorhouse.com
Phone: 1 (800) 839-8640

© 2019 Melissa Monék. All rights reserved.

No part of this book may be reproduced, stored in a retrieval system, or transmitted by any means without the written permission of the author.

Published by AuthorHouse 04/27/2019

ISBN: 978-1-7283-0994-1 (sc)
ISBN: 978-1-7283-0993-4 (e)

Print information available on the last page.

Any people depicted in stock imagery provided by Getty Images are models, and such images are being used for illustrative purposes only. Certain stock imagery © Getty Images.

This book is printed on acid-free paper.

Because of the dynamic nature of the Internet, any web addresses or links contained in this book may have changed since publication and may no longer be valid. The views expressed in this work are solely those of the author and do not necessarily reflect the views of the publisher, and the publisher hereby disclaims any responsibility for them.

DEDICATION

This book is dedicated to every voice that has gone unheard.
To everyone who has a story to tell but have
not yet found the courage to tell it.
To life itself for giving me my struggle.
Without it, I would not be the strong woman I am today.

INTRODUCTION

She opens her book and begins to write her story.
She quickly closes it, because she's afraid of what the world might think.
Afraid to tell her story because she didn't want
the world to see how fucked up she is.
But then she realizes that the world is fucked up too.
She takes a deep breath, reaches deep down, and paints her life
with pen and pad,
which she now calls a Beautiful Disaster.
She is ME and I am HER.
I give to you "Pieces of Me"

PREFACE

A journey of my life, expressed through poetry, Pieces of Me is
a very intimate and personal piece of myself. I now share it with
you. I have been through the mud and damn near jumped off
the cliff. There were times when giving up seemed easier to do.
Things got so bad until being nonexistent felt normal. My pain
and misery was real. So real, until it controlled what would be the
rest of my life. But by God's grace and mercy – He kept me.
I thank Him for this struggle – because without it, I wouldn't
know my own strength. Scared to embrace the poetry in me
because I didn't want the world to see – how fucked up I am. But
then I realized that the world is fucked up too. Afraid I might
not be great – so I was afraid to ever grace any stage – leaving my
words only to each page – of my life. You see – my pen and pad
only got my truth. Now that I'm chasing my passion – I give it to
you – piece by piece. Don't look at me cross eyed. Don't judge me.
Don't even get it twisted. Because I am beautifully damaged.
Pieces of me were shattered everywhere but I needed each
piece – no matter how tainted – to put me back together again.
With each piece, I give you a part of me. By the end of our journey
you will have all of me. As you read, you will understand how
each piece made me whole again. I'm now stronger – wiser –
better. This is my confessional – my release – my therapy.

FOREWORD

The essence of any literary work is when it is concretized in the life of the writer. This has been achieved in this work by my best friend, Melissa Monék Mackey. As her lifelong friend, I can personally chronicle her sojourn from some very dark pits to now a place of solitude. Whether it's pain, despair, hurt, physical and mental abuse, or just loneliness. It does not matter where you are in life or what you have been through this book will give you hope. Everyone will be able to glean some nuggets to help them pick up their shattered pieces from reading this book. We must understand that we have to go through some things in order to become better people. "Pieces of Me" depicts just how strong you can be after the raging storms of life. In this life we live in, as well as this world that we live in, we do not know what the next day holds. We do know that "Shattered Pieces" will prove that you can put your life back together even when it is broken and torn apart. This book is more than a regurgitation of pain. It is a clarion call for all individuals to become educated and dedicated to the proposition that we all must be free. We must be free from more than the physical chains that hold us in one place and hinder us from completing our goals. Melissa Monék Mackey is living proof that when all else fails you must continue to hold on. -Lawana Y. Parrott

FINDING HER WAY BACK

She finds her way back – just to find herself way back.
She looks in the mirror and says – this ain't the me I use to be.
I gotta get out of this darkness and find my way back to me.
But how does she do all of that, when she's buried in so much pain.
How does she conquer anything, when she
feels like there's nothing left to gain.
So the darkness over shadows her and her
past remains a constant reminder.
With no self-esteem or feeling of self-worth left,
at this rate, she'll never find herself.
So giving up seemed so much easier to do than moving on.
She carries a heavy heart – wondering if she'll ever be strong.
She's stricken with awkwardness, embarrassment, and shame.
She clinches tight at the mere mention of her very own name.
Her scars they run deep and her pain even deeper.
She's so broken to the point where she's ready to meet the grim reaper.
Thinking this is her only solution – she's ready to let it all go
because life to her is now just an illusion.
Riddled with humiliation – her transparency she can no longer hide.
She says – why should her flesh have to suffer –
when her soul has already died.
But she still fights – trying to find her way back.
Yet still finding herself way back.
Her struggle is real and the memories are so vivid.
With every session of therapy – she's forced to relive it.

She's fighting for an ounce of joy – a drop of
happiness – and the hope for peace.
She's fighting for closure.
She's fighting for her strength.
Just to give all her pain back to the universe with a burst of release.
And then it happens.
That her that she used to be found her.
It was like looking back in time – at a mirror's image of a younger she.
And the she that found her told her it's time
to release all that negative energy.
The younger she said it's okay now.
Because of you, I'm better.
Because of you, I can now live in peace.
She said thank you for finding the courage to finally release.
And in that moment the mirror images became one.
Because she found her way back.

EVICTED

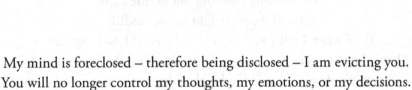

My mind is foreclosed – therefore being disclosed – I am evicting you.
You will no longer control my thoughts, my emotions, or my decisions.
I'm serving you your papers – so find another place to dwell in.
Pack your shit and go!
It's time for you and all your bullshit to exit this door.
I'm serving you notice – and no you don't have three days.
You got to get the fuck on – 'cause here you can no longer stay.
For years you lived rent free and controlled all the space in my head.
Because of you – this damn doctor say I need meds.
What's understood don't need to be explained.
So just get your shit and leave.
You've had me in the choke hold long enough
but now I'm strong enough to come up for air.
It's time for me to breathe.
You caged me up like a bird and clipped my wings.
But now you can miss me with that
because I got the courage of a new song to sing.
For years I let you stay – but today is your day.
And for the first time – ain't shit you can say to make me let you stay.
You had me to believe through all these years
each situation was the same – just with a different cast.
Now that I know better,
I'm evicting your ass!
I beat myself up time after time – and you
were just the thoughts in my head.
I mean – how could I have been so fucked up to be this misled.
You blurred my vision every time I tried to move on.
But moving forward – your ass is gone!

You're Evicted!!!
Fuck sitting your shit out on the curb.
I'm taking it straight to the landfill.
Trust when I tell you – in my head you will no longer live.
Thanks to you – I'm this bipolar depressed shit – the doctor says I am.
But that's okay – because God is elevating me to who I really am.
You're Evicted!!!
I don't need the sheriff or the courts to help put your ass out.
Enough is enough and you will no longer fill me with your doubt.
I've processed.
I've grown.
I've become a better me.
So today – I finally evict you – because I've set myself free.

MY STORY

Everybody in the world got a story to tell.
I only got one so I need you to listen to me well.
I'm a hustler in the hood, not a thief in the night.
I do what I do to make my life right.
It's not all good – no not all the time;
but when it is – watch me shine.
I'm no super hero, wearing a mask or a cape.
I'm just a talented sista trying to get her big break.
I'm no Missy, no Jay-Z, not even a P-Diddy wanna be.
I got my own style.
I got my own creation.
I can drop my lyrics with no hesitation.
My lyrics they flow like that of a river.
When I speak this spoken word,
I will always deliver- what you wanna hear and what you wanna feel.
You see when I speak my words they're coming to you real.
Don't let the looks fool you 'cause what I do, I do well.
I do it to the fullest. I never fail.
Everybody in the world still got their stories to tell;
but I'm still on my first so keep listening to me well.
Forget rags to riches, we went from riches to rags;
that very night when daddy packed his bags.
Being a kid didn't seem so great anymore.
We went from Suburban America to walking through the project's door.
Now what kinda life is this to raise a child?
You can't even sleep at night because everybody's running wild.
Keep listening, I'm not through yet. I've just begun.
You see this is my story, the only one.

The tables turned but it wasn't all that bad.
Life in the projects was just life without dad.
We got older and we understood better.
It made us stronger and taught us how to live together.
But then it happened, mama lost her job, now she's outta work.
And even though I was young, I knew that shit had to hurt.
Three kids, no job, no man; now how she gone work that.
So she turned to public assistance to have her back.
That wasn't good because she became dependent on them;
as if things weren't bad already.
Now ain't this some shit,
the system done became our daddy.
I told you this is my story, my only one.
No more childhood. Good-bye to all the fun.
Found work at the age of 13, even though there were two older than me.
Who would've thought this is how living in the projects would be.
Had to fend for myself and instantly become grown;
'cause mama befriended the streets and left us on our own.
My brother found a way out, now scholarship bound.
My sister found a job to help us with money.
But me, they thought my ideas were funny.
I went to school.
I went to work.
Oh, I also married sports.
I did all I could not to sell myself short.
My story gets deeper and deeper believe it or not.
It had me on the run but for a better plot.
I challenged myself to reach greater heights.
Since this was my story. I knew I wanted a better life.
I found comfort outside of home but it meant me no good.
He was just another nigga from the neighborhood.
He took up the time that took away home's frustration;

but he ended up being more aggravation.
My brother went off to college and my sister
still doing her thing of course.
But me – I was there to witness mama's new addiction, the white horse.
She let herself go and oh how I prayed.
Lord please make her better so we can have better days.
My story goes on along with time.
The older I got, the more I thought I was losing my mind.
Home was no longer home and I felt so alone.
The family I once had was now gone.
We were like strangers to each other – oh what a mess;
because I thought the lesson that we learned was togetherness.
We finished school and boy was I glad.
The only thing on my mind was getting as far
away as I could from the life I had.
I went away to college and experienced better days.
No, I didn't forget where I came from; it helped me make a better way.
I grew, I matured, and I learned a lot.
I was even able to help mama make her addictions stop.
We became closer and the best of friends.
I thank God for giving me mama back again.
This is my story and I'm almost done.
I hope you listened because this is my only one.
Now I'm grown with a family of my own.
I continue the struggle while trying to stay strong.
So as I look back on my life, I give God all the glory.
Because of him, there's a better ending to my life's story.

WALK A MILE IN MY SHOES

How dare you stand there and judge me.
How dare you stand there and just stare.
How dare you even have the nerve to walk a mile in my shoes
when we don't even wear the same size.
You haven't seen the life I lived nor do you know the life ahead of me.
So how can you walk a mile in my shoes.
Have you felt my pain?
Do you know my hurt?
Have you wiped away any of the tears I've cried?
You might wanna rethink walking a mile in these shoes.
Can you withstand life's toughest blow?
Can you bounce back from your hardest fall?
Can you smile at the world while on the inside
you're crying and slowly dying?
Naw, keep them on, don't take 'em off.
Our mile is just beginning.
Submit yourself to humility every time you're in public
because when someone looks at you, you think
they can see right through you.
Their stares peel away at you as they see the abuse you've endured
because you once had your innocence taking away from you.
They see your scars but yet they don't feel your pain.
They see your tears but yet they can't hear your cry.
So who do you tell?
Who can you turn to for help?
Or do you even try?

Walk a mile in my shoes, huh.
Do you think you really can?
Innocence now gone and nothing left of my virtue.
So here I am wondering what's next;
only to find abuse lurking around the corner.
Time and time again, he had his way with me.
The scars he left on my body were nothing
compared to the scars he left on my soul.
You try dealing with being ridiculed in front of your peers
and becoming a stranger to your family and all of society.
Oh, it goes deep.
So deep - that the thought of being dead felt better than being alive.
Afraid to walk, afraid to talk, afraid to even just be,
because I knew at any given moment he'd strike like a snake.
Baby I'm sorry, baby I love you, baby I didn't
mean to was all I'd ever hear.
What the hell!
Nigga, you beat on me like a rug.
You punch on me like a punching bag
and all you can say is baby I'm sorry, I didn't mean to.
Tell that to my limp body, my torn heart, and my broken soul.
Hmph, and you think you can walk a mile in my shoes.
There you are, continuing to stare, placing a label on me.
You don't know what I go through.
You don't know what I've been through.
You don't know me!
Come walk this mile in my shoes and let's see if you still feel the same.
Looking for love but all I knew was hurt.
Why do I keep falling for these dead beat ass niggas
who just keep pounding my face to the dirt.
Awww damn!
I let this one get me caught up.

Now I got a baby on the way.
How in the hell Imma bring another life into this
world when he's fucking me up every day. Do I
keep it, do I flush it, or do I even tell him?
Damn, my whole thought process just went dim.
You don't know me so don't judge me 'cause
you don't know the life I've lived.
Strap them boots up and keep walking.
Let's see if you got my strong will.
Beaten to a pulp - inches from death.
Worried about bringing a baby into this world and I'm dying myself.
Blood everywhere but no one hears my cry.
No matter how much I'm yelling or screaming – I'm left here to die.
Trying to hold on but giving up seemed easier to do.
Oh, I see – you no longer wanna walk a mile in my shoes.
But that's okay because I withstood it all.
No matter what I've been through – I've
bounced back from my hardest falls.
Now the lights off, the rent is due, no gas to keep us warm.
But yet here I am trying to protect a new life in the safety of my arms.
This nigga comes home without a dime to his name.
Lord please rescue me and free me from this pain.
I must be insane to still be around.
I know the whole town is laughing at me like I'm some circus clown.
It's time to pack up what I have and leave this tragedy behind.
There's gotta be something out there better for me that I can find.
Months have passed - a new life and a new me.
I didn't know that this part of walking a mile in my shoes could ever be.
You see everything you took from me I'm gonna take it right back.
You will no longer dictate my life.
All of the abuse that once tore me down has now made me stronger.
My shoes, my mile, my life to live…

Go ahead and take them off now.
You can't live it for me.
Your tough is not my tough.
Your faith is not my faith.
Your strength is not my strength.
I'm here today because I didn't give up.
I didn't let you win.
I walked a mile in my shoes.

DIARY OF ME

From whence I've come,
Who would ever believe that
I experienced so much pain and so much misery.
If you look into the windows of my soul – you'll see the diary of me.
It holds my inner most pain and the scars that you can't see.
It holds all my scared moments and my times of vulnerability.
As I become an open book to the world – I give to you – the diary of me.
Molestation – abuse – mentally and emotionally caged like a bird.
Trying to sing my song – but yet my voice goes unheard.
No one heard my cries.
No one felt my hurt.
No one knew I was suffering in so much pain.
They never knew I was dying on the inside – over and over again.
The advantage you took of me when I was at such a young age.
Made me want to kill you – every time I saw you
because my heart was full of so much rage.
No one to tell but the diary of me,
my life became a complicated hell
and that's who I would be.
You cheated me out of an experience
that I'll never be able to regain.
Now every relationship I have
I fuck it up time and time again.
You made me believe that what you were doing was the norm.
When all you were doing was giving me bodily harm.
I suppressed my past and went on with my life.
But the suppression just made it worse.
Because now every week I have to sit on a therapist couch

putting my life in reverse.
Reliving all the hell that you put me through
And to think you were someone I once looked up too.
A grown ass man.
A predator searching for easy prey.
I wish I had the courage back then to put your ass away.
Instead – with a bleeding heart
I decided to become invisible to the world – not to be seen anymore.
I got so discouraged – I found myself knocking at death's door.
But I now have the strength to tell my story
And because this is the dairy of me – it will have a better ending.

HOMELESS

For 12 months – 52 weeks – 365 days
Me and my kids had no place for our heads to lay.
But if you saw us – you would've never known,
that at the end of each and every day – we had no place to call home.
Family was family – thought I was just looking for a hand out.
Them on the outside looking in
they didn't realize that – we were really out.
From pillow to post – hotel to hotel – for them I had to make it work.
I had to stare my kids in the face every fucking day
While they act like they were good – I saw their true hurt.
Believe it or not they even tried to be strong for me.
When I'm supposed to be their provider
and their sole source of security.
I had to make it work for them but the struggle was real.
I found myself just sitting in my car every night,
crying out to God with my silent tears.
I did this and I did that
And some of those things I'm not proud of at all.
But I had a son and a daughter who didn't deserve any of this.
And for a whole 12 months – 52 weeks – 365 days
This is the life they had to witness.
Some days were better than others.
But at times I felt less than that of a mother.
I even contemplated them being raised by another.
But then I realized that I couldn't do that to them.
So we weathered the storm together.
They gave me the strength and courage to
get out there and make it better.

In December 2009,
I made their faces light up on that Christmas day.
In that very priceless moment
it didn't matter that we had no place to stay.
And in that very same moment,
God was redirecting my life's path.
You see, in January 2010,
He blessed us with our own home to have.
That day was special because it was the very day of my son's birth.
With a smile on his face, he said to me,
no birthday gift will ever beat the worth
of having a place to call home.
With tears in my eyes, I just held him tight.
Because from homeless to happy was our new life.

FROM THE PITS OF HELL

From the pits of hell, God created greatness.
What you see now didn't always look like this.
You see – I done drove through the dirt and swam through the mud.
But God's grace and mercy saved me,
before I drowned in my own flood.
At my weakest point – He made me stronger than ever.
He made me know – that my life story was better.
He pulled me out – brushed me off – and said Melissa go run this race.
He said stop trying to prove your worthiness –
because for you I got a special place.
He said I have a purpose for your life – but you got to run the race.
You see – I chose you as a vessel to be a light in this dark place.
Your struggle has been great – but I designed you to be greater.
Don't let man tell you – you can't – because
there's gonna always be haters.
Don't lose sight on what I've destined you for.
Stop trying to enter those doors that have been closed.
You gotta understand that what I have for you is yours.
Stay strong – because I am your strength.
Stay focused – because I am your guide.
Hold on to my unchanging hand and I will fight your every fight.
My love for you is unconditional and that will never change.
I just need you to believe in yourself – and the power of my name.
From the pits of hell – God – He saved a wretch like me.
He gave me back every dream I ever gave up on,
even the ones you said couldn't be.

He healed those internal scars that life gave to me.
From the pits of hell – I rise.
Stronger than I ever been – ready to conquer this world.
I'm no longer a victim
I am the victor.
I'm walking in my new life that God has purposed me for.
I may have lost a few fights but the battle is mine to win.
I've been blessed with a new finish line and I'm ready to begin.

SHE IS ME

She's crying out to me
But her cries – they go unheard.
She's reaching out to me
But I didn't take her hand.
So she falls back into the shadows of darkness.
Losing herself once again.
She said to me
Melissa – I need you.
I'm tired of being neglected.
You put everyone before me
But I'm the one here for you time after time.
She said she's tired and I had to make a choice.
So I chose HER.
For SHE is ME!
And I love me far more than tis world ever will.
So now we're good and life is great.
I didn't know loving HER could feel like this.
When I look in the mirror, SHE smiles right through me.
SHE stands within me.
SHE holds my head high and sticks my chest out.
SHE got me feeling like I'm the shit.
SHE embraces US and says – see what it
feels like to be in love with YOU.
For SHE is ME – and I'm loving her like never before.
Time goes on – and after all of that – here I
am once again face down in the dirt.
But SHE came along and saved me from MYSELF.
SHE must have known I was about to take my last breath.

I was on the road to destruction,
But SHE loved me enough to catch me every time I fell.
SHE said no – not today – I got you.
Now that shit is REAL!
But with each and every promise,
I broke them every time.
It irritated and frustrated HER because
We are two in the same with one like mind.
SHE took me back to the mirror so I can see HER hurt and pain.
SHE said why do you keep doing this to US?
I hear HER loud and clear but I think it's too late.
It didn't dawn on me that SHE was my saving grace.
HER limp body just lie there with a bleeding heart.
SHE couldn't speak but I heard HER every word.
I try to revive HER but nothing happens.
I tried again and still nothing.
But then it happened.
I cried out to HER and SHE heard me.
I reached out to HER and SHE took my hand.
After all the overlooking and neglect
SHE was still here willing to receive ME.
OUR souls intertwined because WE are one.
I slowly brought HER back to life.
HER heart is playing my favorite song.
I fall in love with HER for real this time.
For SHE is ME and I am HER.
I CHOOSE ME!
So I finally come to my senses and realize what I'm about to lose.
SHE put me back in front of the mirror and said this is for the last time.
I am YOU and YOU are ME!
When you disregard YOU – you disregard ME.
Look at YOU!

You're smart – beautiful – intelligent – vibrant – loving
Caring and passionate about everything that you do.
Stop letting the world tell you different.
I say to HER – how can I when all I've done is fail.
She said to ME – then get back up and keep running this race
Because God isn't through with YOU yet.
SHE stood me up and straightened me out –
and with a big smile on HER face,
SHE embraced me with everything left in HER.
In that very moment I released every
Hurt – harm – abuse and disappointment I ever endured.
I looked in the mirror one last time and we were connected once again.
Loving HER is loving ME.
For I am Her and SHE is ME.
Now I'm happier and SHE is too because I learned to
Love ME with no limits.

LOOK INTO MY EYES

Look into my eyes and tell me what you see.
A product of disaster, naw, that's no longer me.
I got my act together, now I'm rising to shine.
Before it's all over
"The World Will Be Mine."
I've become so focused,
Man – I'm chasing my dreams.
I'm putting the past behind me; it's time to come clean.
As these thoughts race through my mind,
they're driving me wild.
They say I wouldn't make it but I'm on my last mile.
I got a one track mind and I won't be stopped.
No matter how hard you try,
I'm gonna make it to the top.
I'm going full blast.
I feel it in my veins.
This time around, it's not from life's pain.
My childhood – gone....
Nothing of it left to share,
but the pain and the memories of why I was there.
My mind started wandering and I stopped dreaming.
There was nothing in this world again that I could believe in.
So I got tatted up at a very young age.
Thought it would take away the pain but it only built rage.
Rage that I had for everyone who didn't care.
Rage that I had because no one was there.
Then it happened all at once.
I remember that night.

It all flashed before me right before I took my life.
But God stepped in and quickly changed the plan.
He made it all better when he took me by the hand.
You see, a product of a disaster, I will no longer ever be.
Now, look into my eyes and tell me what you see.

COMMON LAW

We can't be fixed!!
Those were the last words she said to me
Before I realized I didn't need to be with this chic.
Because after 15 years of common law marital bliss,
I can't believe she had the nerve to even utter that shit!
So here I am – 3 years later
I'm trying to pick up the pieces to a puzzle that never fit.
I know right – that shit don't make sense.
15 – common
But where's my common sense
As I'm battling to have a healthy relationship.
I mean help me out.
15 – common law – marital – bliss!!!
And she come with this shit 'bout we can't be fixed.
So yeah – here I am 3 years later
I done become one bipolar ass chic….
I got trust issues – and they shouldn't even be with you
Because she the one who fucked me up not you,
But I do….
Ending us before we start – because – I'm protecting my heart.
I'm protecting it from what could be – and scared to let down my guard.
So I find you slipping away because
You don't wanna deal with my bullshit
Because of her bullshit
That I'm making our bullshit – makes sense.
Expecting you to heal wounds and scars you didn't put here.
Finding you – but about to lose you
Because I'm still holding on to bullshit from a 15 year

Common law marital bliss.
You know – the one she said couldn't be fixed.
So I find myself holding on with everything that I got
Because I know everything in my past you're not.
Chipping away at the wall I've built – so you can see my soul.
You see – she thought she had me – when she left me lonely
Leaving my heart with so many holes.
But what she didn't realize is that God
He had a plan for me.
You see in order for me to see the forest –
out of my life – he removed she.
15 – it still rings in my head from time to time.
WE – CAN'T – BE – FIXED!!!
But yet here I am 3 years later – loving who I'm supposed to be with.
Now ain't that some shit?
You see – it took me 18 years to realize
That in 15 years – I couldn't make the pieces to the puzzle fit
But only 3 – to realize she wasn't who I was meant to be with.

BLIND

Right in front of me she stood – with open arms and a loving heart.
But I was too blind to see – from the blurred
vision of my past's emotional scars.
She reached out to me and – I took her hand – but refused her heart
because I predicted what the outcome would be.
And in all truth – she came with no strings
attached – she just wanted me.
Heart pounding – vision blurred – already feeling defeated.
So I did the most obvious – yes – I cheated.
But in my mind I wasn't cheating on her – I was cheating on my past.
But it was her who got hurt by my actions.
I didn't trust her feelings – and – I was too scared to believe her heart.
Afraid of what could be – I ended us before we could start.
Regardless of – she saw something special
within me and stayed through it all.
Blinded by my own insecurities – I let her take the fall.
She got up – brushed herself off – saying with you I will stay.
I know it had to be hell
because I took her on an emotional roller coaster each and every day.
She put up with my bullshit.
She dealt with my mood swings.
But then I got that phone call.
We need to cut ties and move on.
That night I couldn't sleep – the next morning I cried.
Trying to swallow this pill of emotions
because I allowed myself to be blind.
Teary eyes – heavy heart – broken spirit.
I said to her – I made this life – so I have to live it.

I can't believe I let her get away.....
Not a day goes by that I don't wish I could see her face or hear her voice.
I can't believe I jeopardized everything I love
making a poor ass choice.
Blind... I can't see – but yet - my heart is still guiding me.
It's crying out to you.
Can you hear it – or do you even want to at all.
I think she really means it this time
Because the voicemail is what I get every time I call.
The more I apologize – the more I seem to make things worse.
She says how can you say you care for me and did what you did.
Love don't supposed to hurt!!
But I say to her – with every breath that I breathe.
Baby I'm sorry for being so blind.
Please – out of my life – I don't want you to leave.
No longer blind and distracted by my past.
My eyes are open and my heart is too.
I'll do whatever it takes – even if it means living the rest of my life
making it up to you.

YOU CAN'T HURT ME ANYMORE

You took away my innocence like a thief in the night.
Then you tried to comfort it like everything was alright.
You led me to believe that what you were doing to me was okay.
I can't believe I suffered through the pain day after day.
You violated my body time after time.
Said you wasn't worried because if anyone found out,
it would be your word against mine.
How can I fight this, I didn't know what to do.
While all the while my body was being used and abused.
Why didn't I do anything?
Why didn't I say anything?
Why didn't I tell?
At that age I didn't have the courage - so my life became a living hell.
Because of you I lost trust in men and that wasn't hard to do.
You see you left me so torn – my heart continued to accept love's abuse.
For so long you had me trapped in my past still living through the hurt.
I finally got strong enough and built up my nerve.
I built them up enough to tell myself you can't hurt me anymore.
It was now time to sweep all the hurt out the door.
My pain stayed captive for so very long.
But now I got the strength to say - pain be gone!!
You can't hurt me, no not anymore.
Because I'm not that weak child you took advantage of sometime before.
So know that you can no longer ever hurt me again.
I refuse to let that be.
Because I've taken what you've done
and instead of being a victim I'm becoming a better me.

DADE COUNTY

Dade County – Scott Projects born and raised.
But they say don't nothing good come outta Dade.
Born and bred of nothing but greatness,
This Dade County girl is headed to the top.
I'm taking flight and I won't be stopped.
High school graduate – college educated – a teacher by profession.
Now I'm an open book to the world – because I'm chasing my passion.
Artist – Writer – Poet – Published Author
But they say don't nothing good come outta Dade.
Miami, Florida – 305 – I'm Dade County till the day I die.
I was chosen by God – and –
His grace and mercy won't let me fall
Because He don't call the qualified – He qualifies the called.
Some of ya'll didn't get that – but you will on the way home.
But they say don't nothing good come outta Dade.
I fought the fight.
I made it through the struggle.
I beat the odds.
I'm not a statistic.
I'm doing some shit some think ain't realistic.
See – many are called but few are chosen
So – I'm thanking god for putting on this road – and
I'm thanking Him for this chosen path.
You see – my love for this here poetry
got me trying to make to the first round draft.
I'm like put me in the game coach
Take me off the bench
And we just in the first quarter.

I did everything I've ever done because I got a son and a daughter.
I done seen some things.
I've done some things.
Yet still I rise – out of the shadows of darkness.
But they say don't nothing good come outta Dade.
A priceless friend – loyal to the end
But you too busy trying to see what I got – when –
I ain't got shit.
Dade County – Scott Projects born and raised.
But that was back in the days
When friendship and loyalty went a long way.
Your word was all you had.
If you beefed with me – we settled it in the streets.
But not with violence and guns
You see – fights that were fought – were one on one
And believe it or not the best man won.
But check this out – 2 hours later – we were the best of friends again
Not even knowing why we were throwing hands.
So here we are pounding it up – like nothing ever happened
But that was back in the day.
Dade County – Scott Projects born and raised.
But that was back in the days
When kids were kids and we stayed in our lanes.
We didn't talk back – we just mumbled under our breath.
And when those street lights came on
you better believe we scattered like roaches.
Because we had mama's like Roz – Debbie – and Lola
standing on porches.
Don't get it twisted
we fucked up from time to time
but we had sense enough to know – not when to get out of line.
But that was back in the day.

Dade County – Scott Projects born and raised.

But that was back in the days.

When we blocked the streets just so Uncle Al can DJ.

That kinda back in the day – when kids went outside to play.

I mean – play real games like hopscotch –

double dutch – and four square.

But that was back in the day – when kids knew how to play.

Then we wonder why obesity in our kids is on the rise

When they don't even know there's a such thing as a playful outside.

But how can they when there's a homicide on every corner.

Dade County – Scott Projects born and raised.

But they still say don't nothing good come outta Dade.

Yet – still I rise.

This Dade County girl's life got a purpose.

You see – it took a long time – but now I know my self-worth

And not you – you – or even you can take that away from my being.

You can never walk a mile in my shoes

Or see the things I've seen.

69th Terrace right on two – two Ave

This project girl just made it to her first round draft.

So when you look at me – don't tell me what my God can't do

He brought me out of my darkness and he'll do the same for you.

Dade County – Scott Projects born and raised.

Take a good look at me

Because – I'm some of that good that come outta Dade.

BEAUTIFUL DISASTER

I'm boxed in – feel like I can't win
But I'm gone fight till I can't.
See – for me – giving up is not an option….
It's not even a thought.
I mean what you thought
That I was gonna fold and give in.
Sorry to burst your bubble….
But – failure is not in my view
I'm determined to win.
For so long – I've been held captive by own insecurities.
Now I'm full of my own securities.
So – nothing you say – can make me doubt my capabilities.
See – I'm standing on this stage
In front of strangers who love this craft.
See ya'll – ya'll help me break through this
box – and leave it all right here.
Some said I wouldn't make it – but look at it me now!
I'm a beautiful disaster – still standing on His word.
See I'm a visionary – walking in my own vision
So fuck what you heard.
I may not have won all my fights.
But my battle – I will defeat.
I'm that diamond in the rough
That will shine so bright – the next time we meet.
Remember my name….
It's Mel Mo Mac.
I'm an artist – writer – poet – published author.
But my disaster is so beautiful – y'all can't see that.

31

I'm still standing.
I won't break.
I won't bend.
Imma smile to the world – even when it hurts.
If I learned nothing else from life's struggles
I've learned my self-worth.
It's more than that predator making me his prey.
It's more than being homeless for 12 months – 52 weeks – 365 days.
It's more than this bipolar depression that the doctor say….
My self-worth….
It has become everything to me.
It's making me who I am – as I take this self-healing journey.
I've learned to love.
I've learned to live.
I've even learned to forgive
All those who hurt me
Including myself.
So I'm tearing down these walls….
Boxed in I will no longer be.
I'm standing before you – full of my own transparency.
So see right through me – and envision my soul
Take a look into my eyes and watch what they behold.
For I……
I am a Beautiful Disaster – now watch me unfold.

BI

Doctor says, I'm unspecified bipolar depressed.
I really couldn't wrap that around my thoughts,
So I just say
I'm creatively blessed.
Because it takes a whole lot of creativity
to survive the shit I been through.
And if my eyes are the windows to my soul
Then I'll always shut the world out
Just to protect you from what they behold.
I have scars that cut so deep
until my heart doesn't cry anymore…
But the doctor says I can be treated.
What I'm trying to figure out is how do you treat internal scars?
Does he even know the pain that's embedded in my heart?
So I sit on his couch for all of an hour – like
What the hell can this dude tell me that I already don't know?
Does he not know he's wasting his time?
Because he can't fix my emotional broke.
He calls it unspecified bipolar depressed
But bi means two and there's only one me.
Broken, torn, and damaged
But still loving unconditionally.
Mentally and emotionally controlled
By a past full of pain.
But now I'm strong enough to give it back to the universe
Never to return again.
So he treats me with a pill
With a side effect of suicidal thoughts.

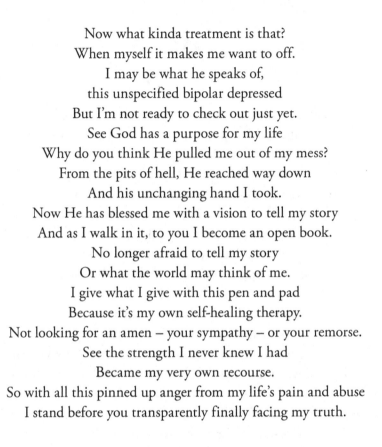

Now what kinda treatment is that?
When myself it makes me want to off.
I may be what he speaks of,
this unspecified bipolar depressed
But I'm not ready to check out just yet.
See God has a purpose for my life
Why do you think He pulled me out of my mess?
From the pits of hell, He reached way down
And his unchanging hand I took.
Now He has blessed me with a vision to tell my story
And as I walk in it, to you I become an open book.
No longer afraid to tell my story
Or what the world may think of me.
I give what I give with this pen and pad
Because it's my own self-healing therapy.
Not looking for an amen – your sympathy – or your remorse.
See the strength I never knew I had
Became my very own recourse.
So with all this pinned up anger from my life's pain and abuse
I stand before you transparently finally facing my truth.

JOURNAL NOTES

Dear journal
You're the only one who knows my inner most thoughts.
When my pen meets your paper - my mask - it comes off.
You get what the world cannot yet handle.
You get the worst of me and you still let me vent all over you.
I can give you my truth and walk away   .
knowing it's gonna stay right here with you.
As I speak to you - my tears – they moisten your lines.
Because I give you my truth and what hurts on the inside.
The world looks at me and sees someone who's got their shit together.
But if they got what you get – then they'd really know better.
The world gets the mask that smile every day.
They don't know the mental and emotional struggle
I go through just to make a way.
They can't feel my pain or even see my scars.
They can't even begin to understand the brokenness of my heart.
But you,,,,,
You've been here with me and know all of my deep dark secrets.
You've been here through my ups and downs – my good and bad
Even when I made suicide the only option I had.
So I ask you journal,
since you've been through it all with me.
Do you think the world is ready?
I got a story to tell and it's my own self-healing therapy.
So whether they're ready or not
it's time I release all the pieces of me.
I know it won't be easy.
I'm not looking for praises or applause.

You see I'm doing this just because.
Because – I need to move on
from my past - and take it all back.
I release all of my hurt – pain – anger and abuse
to the universe never to return again.
No longer afraid of what the world may think.
I'm not doing this for the world – I'm doing it for me.
Now brave enough to make my journal notes
my story – my life – my release.
Because
I'm no longer living in my shadows of darkness.
I'm finally at peace.

I GOT A STORY TO TELL

I got a story tell – and I ain't the one to gossip –
so – you can say you heard from me.
Oh – I got a story to tell – about how Jesus died up on Calvary.
I got a story to tell – about the one who set me free.
You see – I got a story to tell – about how He saved little old me.
He didn't have to do it – but yet He did.
He sacrificed His only son – so a sinner like me can live.
Oh – I got a story to tell – because of all the great things He's done.
You see – you don't know the dark roads I've traveled and
The places He's brought me from.
From a sinner to a saint – that will probably never be me.
But with the story I tell – you'll never question my Christianity.
I've seen a lot and done a lot – most of it I'm not proud of.
But the one thing that I know – is that I'm forgiven with my
Father's agape love.
You see – I got a story to tell – and it's one I know so very well.
Take it for what it's worth – our Father – He never fails.
No – I can't quote scripture after scripture
but my testimony tells my story.
You will never understand why I give Him all the glory.
I got a story to tell that should've ended with me in a grave.
But – oh – how excellent – He made death behave.
I got a story to tell that should've ended with me in somebody's jail.
But God's grace and mercy always prevail.
I got a story to tell that should've ended with me
holding that knife in my hand – that lonely night.
But my Father quickly intervened – and said no my child
I have a purpose for your life.

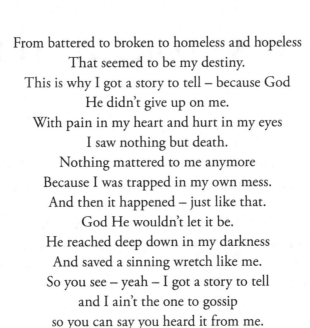

From battered to broken to homeless and hopeless
That seemed to be my destiny.
This is why I got a story to tell – because God
He didn't give up on me.
With pain in my heart and hurt in my eyes
I saw nothing but death.
Nothing mattered to me anymore
Because I was trapped in my own mess.
And then it happened – just like that.
God He wouldn't let it be.
He reached deep down in my darkness
And saved a sinning wretch like me.
So you see – yeah – I got a story to tell
and I ain't the one to gossip
so you can say you heard it from me.

THE EPIDEMIC

Hey baby,

What's up? Thanks for bringing me into your life. Now that I'm here,
I'm yours forever. I'm gonna give you hell. See, let me explain. When
you let Keith into your life, you opened your doors to a world of me.
He brought to you joy, happiness, love, and oh did I mention, me. He
got me from Sharon, who picked me up from Ron, who exchanged me
with Mary. It's funny how I travel 'cause I have no particular targets.
No, no, I don't discriminate. Man, woman, or child; Jamaican, Haitian,
or Caucasian. I have no preference. You see, I'm as smooth as Keith
was to you but as deadly as crack to a fiend. I have no remorse. I feel
no love. I'll dismiss you from this world and go on about my business
like nothing's happened. I don't care about you. I don't love you. Now
that you've got me, you can share me with others or you can keep me to
yourself. I love to be shared and everyone is always spreading me around.
Soon, I will not only control you but everyone Keith is with after you. I
own you. You can't get rid of me. No one can. I can turn your life into
your worst nightmare. What did you think? I'd let Keith enjoy you and
me not get a piece of the action. Think again. So, now what are you
going to do? Be mad at Keith, be mad at you, or be mad at me. Hell,
what can you do? You allowed me into your life by being uneducated
and illiterate to me. It's not like you didn't know about me, I'm on every
billboard; almost on every corner. I'm on every other T.V. commercial.
And oh, how I like to see my name in print. People like you; I love to
come in contact with. Blind to my facts but yet you can see it all. Too
bad you didn't see me coming. Don't get me wrong, I'm not picking on
you. You're just my most recent victim. Besides, I didn't choose you; you
chose me when you decided to lay with Keith unprotected. Next time-
oh, there won't be a next time. I'm gonna break you down so bad no one

will be able to recognize you. First I'm gonna take your appetite. Then I'll break down your immune system, leaving you vulnerable for every other germ out there. Next, I'll disable the use of your arms and legs, leaving your body limp. And before I end it all, I'll take away your sight, leaving you with nothing more to see but the last memories of me. And finally, like a thief in the night, I will rob you of the rest of your life. Don't fuck with me. My name is AIDS and I will kill you!!!!

I WROTE YOU
THIS LETTER

Dear Mama
I was just sitting here thinking about you.
You know it's been a decade – but it feels like just
yesterday we were laughing on the phone together.
I miss you so much – I decided to write you this letter......
By the time you get this message I hope you're doing fine.
Just wanted to let you know you're on my mind.
10 years have passed already so soon.
I mean just the other day we had a lunch date at noon.
A walk in the park – a trip to the store
Mama, we had dinner and a movie and so much more.
Why couldn't time wait?
Why did you have to leave?
Mama, I wish you were here to witness me accomplish all of my dreams.
I know you're watching from heaven up above
'cause no matter what I'm going through I can feel your love.
It embraces me and keeps my spirit warm.
I make it through each and every day in the comfort of your arms....
Everyone is doing fine and so am I – but I'm still stuck with the question
Mama, I'll always ask why.
Why couldn't you stay?
Why can't you be here?
It's hard getting by but I smile through the tears.
I toss and turn. I cry myself to sleep.
I stay up late at night with the hopes that you'll come see me.
Then I hear your voice whisper in my ear

baby don't fret 'cause Mommy's always right here.

I'm by your side. I'll never leave.

My flesh may be gone but my spirit will always be.

In that moment – I feel the comfort of your embrace.

And I'm thanking God because I know you're in a better place.

Even though time has passed – the memories – they live on.

At times I get weak while trying to stay strong.

Rest well my Queen – because through me you will always live on.

You see my heart plays a lot of beats but you're forever my favorite song.

You live in my heart each and every day.

Mama, I get so discouraged sometimes – but I try to keep the faith.

The faith that one day I'll see you once more

and that'll be the day when we meet at heaven's door.

When I get there – the first question from me will be

has anyone seen Roslyn Gail Mackey?

I'll run into your arms – and hear you whisper

Melissa, I'm so proud of you – job well done.

So this will never be good-bye, just see you later.

Because when we meet again

I know it'll be so much greater.

As I move forward in this life,

I will always remember our bond

that of a mother and daughter.

Mama, no matter what, you'll always be my bridge over troubled waters.

I Love You Mrs. Roz!!

SUICIDAL THOUGHTS

These four walls....
They talking – and they talking – and they talking.
These four walls...
They getting closer – and closer – and closer.
Pills on the bed – razor in her hand
These four walls....
They're making her not want to ever wake up again.
Closing from the right – the left – the front – the back.
Now the ceiling 'bout to cave in.
Her heart is hurting so bad
until she's made giving up her only option.
Life – life – life....
Death – death – death....
She's fighting for the obvious
but she's about to take her last breath.
No one to call.
No one to talk to.
No one to stop her from drowning in her pain.
No one to hold her and comfort her
letting her know there's sunshine after the rain.
Her mind is all over the place.
She can't focus.
She can't think.
She can't get these thoughts outta her head.
She opens the pill bottle....
But in that moment – she reaches for hope instead.
She cries out
Father can you hear me – please help me ease the pain.

I wanna be happy.
I can't keep reliving this – over and over again.
The pills pour out – the razor still held in her hand.
But God steps in – because for her – he had a better plan.
He said to her – no my child – I won't let you do it this way.
I have purposed your life – so hold on
for tomorrow will be a better day.
The bottle hits the floor.
The razor drops from her grip.
She takes herself on a mental trip.
Releasing each moment of hurt – harm – and danger
She becomes a stranger…to what use to be.

THE DEPTHS
OF MY SOUL

The depths of my soul – will forever behold….
The scars that life has put on me.
Broken – torn – damaged
But like a tree rooted in the ground – I will not bend.
I have found my strength from within – to finally begin….
That process of healing without being afraid.
Here I stand – transparent and true….
Pouring out my heart to those who never knew.
My pain and suffering
Made me stronger – made me better – made me whole
Enabling my soul to finally behold – and embrace that who I am.
No longer afraid of my truth – now I give it to you.
Courage has made me strong.
Strength has allowed me to fight.
Fighting has made me a winner.
Now I'm at the begin of…. A new me.
The depths of my soul – still behold the scars that you cannot see.
See – many didn't make it – but your girl – I'm still here.
I'm fighting my best fight.
I'm running this race and beating the odds
Because I know at the end of the tunnel – there is a light.
You tried to break me – but God kept me together.
You tried to tear me to pieces – but God is my glue.
You tried to damage me – but you can't – because
God is my light and my truth.
See you – you thought you destroyed me – when you left my soul to die.

You thought you tarnished me – when you
slandered my name with so many lies.
You thought I would just give up – give in – and throw in the towel.
But I don't know how…. When I'm a fighter.
The depths of my soul is still trying to behold
But my strength won't let that be.
I'm gonna fight 'til I can't
Because a winner – that's who I am inside of me.

TRUST ISSUES

Lying in your truth – still feeling the wrath of his abuse.
I'm trying to embrace your love – but – I got trust issues.
So let me cruise on in this breeze – while my heart is at ease.
Because – learning to love me – hasn't been easy.
The scars you can't see – they run deep into my soul
keeping me on the run – from what true love may behold.
You see – I was quick to love.
Easy to give – never to see it coming.
So please forgive me – if I mistake your gentle stroke for an abrupt strike.
Please excuse me – if I mistake your gentle kiss for a venomous bite.
Breathing hasn't been easy – but – now that my heart is cruising
It just wants to enjoy the breeze.
Now you say you wanna love me – but – love
for me has only been bodily harm.
So if I seem alarmed – please understand – I got trust issues.
I hear your words – and I truly want to believe – but
this heart of mine has to see in order to receive….
Anything that can be true.
Once broken….shattered….torn down and made to believe….
that the only love I was worth – was a man putting his hands on me.
Confined to worthlessness – humility – and shame.
How can I have been less of a woman – to let my heart take the blame.
So as I lie in your truth – my tunnel vision won't let me see your truth
because I got trust issues.
But there's no doubt in my mind that – we seem like such a great fit.
But my heart is scared.
It needs to feel loved – needed – and wanted….
Not beaten – battered – and taunted…. By past abuse.

Now do you really wanna love me – and
become everything you say I need?
Are you sure you wanna take this ride and explore the brokenness in me?
Because I've been left alone so many times
leaving my soul to die.
Left alone so many times – living a life full of so many lies.
So you see – you can't only promise me
you have to also promise my heart
that the love you have won't end in scars.
'Cause even after all that I've been through
I don't see myself waking up to anyone else.
My heart is on this cruise – but now that you're here
I don't wanna keep doing this by myself.
Know that my fear is strong – but – I really more than like you.
So if I'm dreaming – please let me continue to sleep.
'Cause I'm lying in your truth – finally ready to let go of my trust issues.
I wanna take this cruise with you – and together feel the breeze.
For once – I want that kinda love – that will allow my heart to breathe.

THE LIVING PROOF

The song writer says
You thought I was worth saving – so you came and changed my life.
You thought I was worth keeping – so you cleaned me up inside.
You thought I was to die for – so you sacrificed your life
So I could be free – free to tell everyone I know....
That on that day some 25 years ago.
You stepped in and saved me from myself
with razor in my hand and nothing but the thoughts of death.
You stopped my process because you saw in
me more than I could ever see.
You took my wounded heart and began to potter this clay
even though you knew my flesh would still go astray.
I thank you for being a God of another
chance – not just a second chance
Because without it where would I be?
Probably still broken – torn – and damaged
allowing life to get the best of me.
So I believe the song writer when he says
You thought I was worth saving – so you came and changed my life.
You thought I was worth keeping – so you cleaned me up inside.
You thought I was to die for – so you sacrificed your life.
So I could be free – free to tell everyone I know....
That on that day some 15 years ago – when I sold my soul to the devil
You wouldn't let it be.
I was being dragged through the dirt and swimming in the mud
But you – you never judged.
I was more harm to myself than anyone could ever be.
But once again – you saved me – from me.

Standing on that cliff – staring death right in the face.
You quickly intervened and said – my child
Now is not the time – and this is definitely not the place.
You said fear not – I got you covered and I
have a purposed life waiting for you.
And in that moment – you changed the outcome to all my life plans.
I took that leap of faith and decided to hold
on to your unchanging hand.
So yeah – I still believe the song writer when he says
You thought I was worth saving – so you came and changed my life.
You thought I was worth keeping – so you cleaned me up inside.
You thought I was to die for – so you sacrificed your life.
So I could be free – free to tell everyone I know….
That on that early morning night – some 10 years ago
When you called my mother home to her final resting place
I lost my best friend and the only one who grew to understand my pain.
Life began to have no meaning – once I
realized I would never see her again.
My stubbornness wouldn't let me mourn – it
just drove me crazy over time.
I became a ticking time bomb – I damn near lost my mind.
But you let me know – that no weapon formed against me will prosper
As long as I have you on my side.
And with that – some 5 years ago – you completely changed my life.
You see it took a long time to get here – but it was well worth the wait….
That's why on this very day – I can truly say
that you did the unthinkable – you never gave up on me.
Because of your sea of forgetfulness
I am no longer ashamed to tell the world who is
Melissa Monék.
I stand before you – overcoming every inflicted and non-inflicted
hurt – harm – and abuse.
I am God's testimony – I am the living proof!

FRAMED

I've been framed
Into a family of Love, Lies, Secrets, and Deceit.
Just like a picture – I've been captured
But the family's frame has never been complete.
Now shattered to pieces
The glass of Love falls.
Now there is no longer walls…
To this picture frame.
BOOM!
The glass hits the floor
Love opens its door
And – his pour all over me.
One hand over my mouth
The other around my neck.
I wish you would scream – he tells me.
Frame falling apart – because his love would now never depart.
Now every inch of my soul – wish it would
Become a part of that wood – in the frame
That holds that perfect picture – of a broken family.
Because they never heard my cries
Wouldn't believe my words
Too blinded by his lies.
So paint a pretty picture and put it in a frame.
Call it Love – because I've been framed
Into a family of Love, Lies, Secrets, and Deceit.
Just like a picture – I've been captured
But the family's frame has never been complete.
Now shattered to pieces

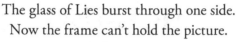

The glass of Lies burst through one side.
Now the frame can't hold the picture.
Lie #1
A perfectly painted picture of mama working so diligently
So how did she find the time to work these streets so whoringly?
She thought we didn't know – because it was never spoke of
But the lies ran through her veins
Escaping through her drug injected arms.
Lie #2
There's a power outage in the neighborhood
But out lights are the only ones off.
Frame that into your picture – and let the reality set in.
Hmph…
Candles for lights, 'cause not even a generator can reignite…
The humility that me and my siblings endure.
Lie #3
You said you'd be here tomorrow – but tomorrow never came.
So like that picture in the frame – I'm left hanging.
And now I will never see another tomorrow with you
Because they covered up your lies.
You see – I know you broke family ties – to go start another one.
I'm just a kid, huh…
I'll never understand.
Well tell that to the broken heart you left me holding in my hand.
Playing father with them – but I call you daddy…
Maybe I shouldn't anymore – 'cause you chose to walk out that door
Leaving our lives unframed.
So paint a pretty picture and put it in a frame
Call it disappointment – cause I've been framed.
Into a family of Love, Lies, Secrets, and Deceit.
Just like a picture – I've been captured
But the family's frame has never been complete.

Now shattered to pieces
The glass of Secrets whisper in the air.
Shhh...
She can never know – or it will tear her apart.
The lies of this secret will break her fragile heart.
But what about me?
Do I even get a say?
His secrets – no secret when I live it every day.
You can never say anything – are the constant words I hear
Because they still believe his truth.
But this dude – her brother – my uncle
Had his way with me – stripping me of my virtue!
So like the picture in a frame – the secrets are held into a four sided space
Locked away unsafely – when every day I have to see his face.
So paint a pretty picture and put it in a frame
Call it shameless – because I've been framed
Into a family of Love, Lies, Secrets, and Deceit.
Just like a picture – I've been captured
But the family's frame has never been complete.
Now shattered to pieces
The glass of Deceit lands at my feet.
No longer knowing who to trust
Knowing my truth has become a must.
The picture no longer hangs in that perfect frame...
The family has lost it because I'm not that little girl anymore.
They say speaking my truth will defame...
The family's perfectly – unperfect picture because
it will no longer fit in the frame.
But my words need to be heard – because they're not listening.
That frame has fallen apart – and just like any unfinished work of art
It just sits there.
Hanging in the balance of what's real and what's fake.

All the Love, Lies, Secrets, and Deceit
I can no longer take.
I've been captured for so long – but in this frame I don't belong.
So paint a pretty picture and put it in a frame.
Call it freedom – 'cause I'm no longer framed
Into a family of Love, Lies, Secrets, and Deceit.
I'm no longer captured and my frame is now complete.

ACKNOWLEDGEMENTS

Father I thank you for the gifted vision you've blessed me with.
I thank you for allowing my works to come to fruition.
As I continue this journey, I will hold on to your unchanging hand.
To my offspring, Domonique and Daniel
I thank God for allowing me to be the vessel to your
existence. You two have witnessed a lot of my struggles as
well as my successes. Even though we've had our share of
ups and downs, thank you for being great children.
It's been a pleasure watching you grow into adults.
Domonique, thank you for my two beautiful
grandchildren, Quantez and Nala.
They have imprinted on my life a love I never thought I could feel.
I love each one of you with my whole heart.
To my siblings Daniel, Cassandra, Damian, Anthony, and Brian
Thank you for epitomizing the definition of family. We may not always
see eye to eye but you guys are always there when it matters the most.
I love you guys to the moon and back. Thank
you for being my greatest supporters.
To my aunt's Clarissa, Valencia, Betty, and Debbie
You four are the closest people I have that keep
me close to my mother and father.
Clarissa and Valencia, you are my mother's oldest and youngest siblings
and I thank you for all the support and wisdom you bestow on me.
Betty and Debbie, you are my father's oldest and youngest siblings.
I thank you two for loving and supporting me
as your own through all of my mess.
They say we can't pick and choose our family
so I'm thankful to God for making you guys mine.

I love you guys more than you'll ever know.
To my poetic family, my fans, and my followers
You guys keep me inspired. Your support has
been nothing less than amazing.
When I decided to embrace the poetry in me, you guys
allowed me a platform to share my voice. Thank you for
loving the craft and embracing me as I journey through it.
Without you, there is no audience for me to be who I am.
Thank you, thank you, thank you!!
To my Best Friend, Lawana Parrott
For the past 30 plus years you have been
my friend, my sister, my support system, and my confidant.
Thank you for being the true meaning of a Best Friend.
You have seen me at my best times and my worst
times and your loyalty never wavered.
I thank you for that. I love you my friend.
To the woman who made a great impact in my life,
my Emily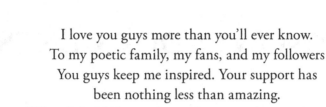
You came into my life when I was at one of my weakest points.
You could have easily walked away knowing everything you knew,
but instead you decided to take a chance on me.
I have experienced love on so many levels and in so many ways, but you,
you took my heart and did the unthinkable with it.
You showed it how to accept love and for that, I thank you.
Thank you for always supporting me and my dreams
and for being one of my biggest fans and supporters.
I thank you for our special kind of love,
our friendship and most of all, all that we have shared together.
-Melissa Monék

ABOUT THE AUTHOR

Melissa Monek, a native of Miami, Florida is an artist, writer, poet, and educator. As she continues her journey from her first published book, M.O.T.H(Matters of the Heart), she begins to depict an insight of her life through poetry. In this unique way, Melissa decided to put a twist on speaking her voice, using this platform to hopefully reach and inspire those who haven't yet found the courage to tell their story.

She know how it feels to be in dark places with no one to turn to, to wear scars that no one can see, and to bear the pain of life with her head held high and a smile on her face.

She is truly a testimony of her many tests. A conqueror, a fighter, a survivor are all the titles that Melissa wear as she continues to press forward on her own self healing journey. Everyday isn't a bad day but when they are, she holds on to God's unchanging hand and weather the storm.

She defines herself as a Beautiful Disaster, a Diamond in the rough that will shine so brightly with everyone she meets.

Printed in the United States
By Bookmasters

Printed in the United States
By Bookmasters